AMAZÔNIA

Colin Teevan and Paul Heritage

AMAZÔNIA

OBERON BOOKS
LONDON

First published in 2008 by Oberon Books Ltd
521 Caledonian Road, London N7 9RH
Tel: 020 7607 3637 / Fax: 020 7607 3629
e-mail: info@oberonbooks.com
www.oberonbooks.com

A catalogue record for this book is available from the British
Library.

ISBN: 978-1-84002-895-9

Cover design by viewdesignstudio.co.uk

Characters

CHICO MENDES

SEU ANTÔNIO, the Master

RICARDO, his nephew

ROSAMARIA, his daughter

CATARINA, his servant

FRANCISCO, his farmhand

TIA TEREZA

VAQUEIRO, a cowboy

SERINGUEIRA, a rubber-tapper

PESCADOR, a fisherman

THE BOTO, a pink dolphin

THE BOI, a bull

DOCTOR

PRIEST

VILLAGERS

Amazônia was first performed at the Young Vic
on 27 November 2008, with the following cast:

BOI / BOTO, Diogo De Brito Sales
CHICO MENDES, Daniel Cerqueira
SERINGUEIRA / MOON, Meline Danielewicz
SEU ANTONIO, Jeffery Kissoon
ROSAMARIA, Daisy Lewis
PESCADOR, Tyrone Lopez
RICARDO, Chris New
VAQUEIRO, Wale Ojo
CATARINA, Golda Rosheuvel
TIA TEREZA, Amanda Symonds
FRANCISCO, Simon Trinder
MUSICIANS Felipe Karam, Anselmo Netto, Gui Tavares

Director Paul Heritage
Associate Director Joe Hill-Gibbins
Design Gringo Cardia
Lighting Philip Gladwell
Choreography and Movement Direction Jean Abreu
Music Direction Santiago Posada
Sound Dan Jones
Stage Manager Suzanne Bourke
Costume Supervisor Catherine Kodicek
Casting Sam Jones CDG
Producer Debra Hauer

Act One

SCENE 1

Enter CHICO. *His shoe squeaks. He takes off his shoe and examines it.*

CHICO

Rubber. Rubber soles. Funny stuff, rubber. Magic stuff. Makes everything from tyres and trainers to the rubbers at the end of your pencil. That's where it got its name. Does anyone know where rubber comes from? (*Response.*) From the juice of the rubber tree. And do you know where the rubber tree comes from? (*Response.*) From Amazônia. I suppose for most of us the story of Amazônia begins with rubber. I'm Chico, and I'm from Amazônia and it all began for me with rubber too. I was a *seringueiro*, I used to drain the rubber latex from the rubber trees. From the time I was a boy I'd walk a huge circuit through the rainforest. I know the forest like I know my own hand, it's the blood that flows through my veins, there is a map of it in my heart. Will I show you? (*Goes to open shirt.*) Unfortunately it's on the inside of my heart. Maybe later. Rubber was the reason Europeans first came to the Amazon and why Brazilian workers moved there, to get as much rubber as they could. Back then rubber was the big thing. Like gold, and it was like a goldrush. Everyone wanted it. But then a Englishman named Henry Wickham snuck into the Amazon and stole a thousand seeds back to London. His shoes didn't make a squeak as he sneaked off. First you'd rubber trees in Kew Gardens in London, and then they were growing them in Malaysia on huge rubber plantations. That was the beginning of the problem for my forest. You started making your own rubber and you didn't need ours. Do you have forests where you come from? (*Response.*) Are they so big that you could walk for months and months and never reach the other side? (*Response.*) What country are you from? (*Response.*) England? Do you know Mr Henry Wickham? Well you tell him from me if you see him – (*Response.*) O you don't. Do you know Mr William Shakespeare? (*Response.*) I do.

'And never since the middle summer's spring
Met we on a hill, in dale, forest, or mead,
To dance our ringlets to the whistling wind,
But with thy brawls though hast disturbed our sport.
Therefore the winds, piping to us in vain,
As in revenge have sucked up from the sea
Contagious fogs which, falling in the land,
Hath every pelting river made so proud
That they have overborne their continents.
The ox hath therefore stretched its yoke in vain,
The ploughman lost his sweat, and the green corn
Hath rotted ere his youth attained a beard...'

Midsummer's Night Dream. You see, you English took our rubber seeds, but we took your Mr Shakespeare in return. And he wrote a lot about forests. And our forest like his forest is all out of season with itself. That's why I have come back. To warn them. The people who live here in Amazônia. To help them. Because tonight is no ordinary night, it's Midwinter's night, that's right, June 23rd. The Feast of São João, Saint John. It's when every year across Brazil they dance the *bumba meu boi*, and ask Saint John's help for the coming year. And here come the villagers of Todos Os Santos with their bull to dance their *bumba meu boi.*

A whistle blows off stage.

SCENE 2

Enter ANTÔNIO, the Master, followed by all the VILLAGERS. ANTÔNIO blows his whistle.

ALL

(*Sung.*) Tonight we come together
To celebrate o *bumba meu boi*,
We're here tonight for the *Festa de São João*.
Sing family, sing friends,
Sing Todos Os Santos,
Bumba meu boi,
Bumba meu boi.

Dance my bull, dance,
Dance my bull, dance!

ANTÔNIO

(*Spoken.*) Sing Ricardo, sing my nephew,
Sing the *bumba meu boi*.

RICARDO

(*Sung.*) On the ranch by the river,
Our Master's bull will dance the festa,
A force of nature, to celebrate São João.
(*Spoken.*) O what a beast!

ANTÔNIO

(*Spoken.*) Sing Rosamaria, sing my daughter,
Sing *bumba meu boi*.

ROSAMARIA

(*Sung.*) And when that great bull bellows,
I feel the earth beneath me tremble.
Oh Amazônia, I hear my heart beat louder.

RICARDO

(*Spoken.*) Oh what a beast!

ANTÔNIO

Sing Catarina, sing Francisco,
Sing my faithful servants.

CATARINA / FRANCISCO

(*Sung.*) São João, São João,
Santo padroeiro,
Bless us on our land.
Bless us on our land.
Accept our humble land.
Accept our humble land.

TIA TEREZA

(*Sung.*) O what a beauty! O what a beast!
Light your fire,
Feel the rhythm of our drums of São João.

ANTÔNIO

(*Spoken.*) Protect our community,
Deliver us from our enemies.

ANTÔNIO whistles.

The Gathering.
Call forth the bull.

Whistle.

ROSAMARIA

Come bull,
Bull of the bright morning,
Come with God and Our Lady.

ALL

Come bull,
Come King of the Union,
Rise up from the cold ground.

ROSAMARIA

Come bull,
Let me lead you
With love to the altar.

ALL

Come bull,
Come King of the Union,
Rise up from the cold ground.

ROSAMARIA

Come bull,
Come rise up from the dead,
And let me show you to these people.

ALL

Come bull,
Come King of the Union,
Rise up from the cold ground.

The procession reaches the altar. ANTÔNIO *blows his whistle.*

ANTÔNIO

São João, we've kept our promise;
Here is your dancing bull.
Bless us, São João, that our small farm might thrive.

ALL

São João hear our prayers.
Now dance bull dance!

ROSAMARIA

That we might know the world and sing it.

ALL

São João hear our prayers.
Now dance bull dance!

RICARDO

That we might hold the world in our hands.

ALL

São João hear our prayers
Now dance bull dance!

CATARINA

That our lives might be sweet,
That we might have enough to eat.

ALL

São João, hear our prayer.
Dance bull dance!

Beat.

ALL

Dance bull, dance!

ANTÔNIO

Dance bull, I said!

Pause. The BULL does not dance. The music stops. Pause.

And still he will not dance! The bull has always danced before. What can be done? Who is to blame? Francisco? What has happened? Francisco!

Anticipating ANTÔNIO's response, exit FRANCISCO. The BULL sees CHICO and is startled, charging around the stage knocking into people, causing mayhem.

Francisco! Where is my *pião* Francisco?

RICARDO

He was here a moment ago, Uncle.

The BULL is brought under control.

ANTÔNIO

Catarina, where has that husband of yours gone to?

CATARINA vomits.

Your costume Catarina! We need to dance the *bumba meu boi*, we need São João's blessing this year more than ever –

RICARDO

It was Rosamaria, Uncle.

ROSAMARIA

What was?

RICARDO

The way she was dancing, she excited the bull. It wasn't right.

ROSAMARIA

You're not right, Cousin Ricardo, haven't you ever seen a woman dance?

ROSAMARIA dances provocatively in front of RICARDO. The other VILLAGERS enjoy it.

RICARDO

Except you're not a woman.

ANTÔNIO

Where did you learn such things, Rosamaria? Get back to the house!

ROSAMARIA

You treat me like a *japiim* you've caught and locked in a cage.

ANTÔNIO

Catarina, take Rosamaria back to the house this instant. And she's not to leave it until I find someone of whom I approve to marry her to.

ROSAMARIA

You can lock up a magic bird, but you cannot stop it singing.

CATARINA vomits again, then escorts ROSAMARIA to the house.

ANTÔNIO

And tidy yourself up, Catarina. Now where is my *pião* Francisco?

TIA TEREZA

Yesterday it wouldn't come out, today it won't dance. (*She looks at CHICO.*) It senses something, that something's wrong.

ANTÔNIO

Francisco!

VAQUEIRO

And the *Festa de São João* is over tomorrow.

TIA TEREZA

If he doesn't dance it's an omen –

VAQUEIRO

We've only got until midnight tomorrow.

TIA TEREZA

An omen. It will be a bad year.

SERINGUEIRA

We'll lose our bull dance like we're losing our rubber trees.

TIA TEREZA
There's not another village in this region that still dances the *bumba meu boi*. We're the only ones.

SERINGUEIRA
That's because the others have been cleared for the roads and the cattle and the soya crops.

TIA TEREZA
The bull senses what's coming.

ANTÔNIO
It's not an omen, it won't be a bad year, because the bull will dance. Francisco!

VAQUEIRO
But why is our herd just skin and bone?

PESCADOR
Why are there hardly any fish in the river?

SERINGUEIRO
Why every week are more of my trees cut down?

RICARDO
Because there is too little pasture land, because of the pollution of the river, because of the illegal logging of the trees. It's the future and it's coming this way.

VAQUEIRO
It's because you fishermen have polluted the river.

PESCADOR
It's because you *vaqueiros* have destroyed the land.

SERINGUEIRA
It's not, it's because you all have destroyed the forest.

ANTÔNIO
Stop, stop bickering all of you! Our *boi* will dance for São João tomorrow night, I tell you, and all shall be well with the forest, the farm and our village. We're not like the others. The diggers will never come here. We'll protect our village and protect our bull.

TIA TEREZA

But it's no wonder it won't dance, Seu Antônio, look at the state of our *festa* clothes. How can we dance the bull dance or the *quadrilha* in these old things? No wonder São João won't bless us this year.

VAQUEIRO

São João has abandoned us. That's why we are so poor.

RICARDO

It's because we need to clear the forest, Uncle, and modernise like all the other farms have done.

ANTÔNIO

No. No, we must do as we have always done. Nor has São João abandoned us. But perhaps you are right Tia Tereza, perhaps we insult him with our efforts. Look at our costumes, listen to the music, and our singing and dancing. Shocking, shameful, shambolic. Yes. This is why the bull won't dance. Women, you must fix the clothes, fix them and wash them for tomorrow night. Make them worthy of Saint John. Musicians, you need to practise. Off the beat and out of tune. Practise all night, practise till your fingers bleed if you need to, but get it right. And the rest of you, sing, sing and dance while you go about your work. I'll go find Francisco. He'll dance all night with the bull if he has to. I give you my solemn undertaking, we'll dance the *bumba meu boi* before midnight tomorrow, or my name's not Antônio Cícero Machado dos Santos Pinheiro e Pinheiro!

TIA TEREZA

What about the bull's crown? It's been crushed in the stampede.

ANTÔNIO

I shall see to the bull's crown, Tia Tereza. Come, my *boi*, let's find that Francisco! Now everyone else, to work. Ricardo…

RICARDO

Yes Uncle?

ANTÔNIO

I believe we too still have a few skin and bone cattle of our own to herd.

RICARDO

Yes Uncle, of course Uncle. As the Master said, everyone to work.

Exit RICARDO and VILLAGERS. ANTÔNIO goes to exit.

CHICO

Master of ceremonies? Master of disharmony more like!

ANTÔNIO

Excuse me, Seringueiro, but do you know who I am?

CHICO

You are Seu Antônio Cícero Machado dos Santos Pinheiro e Pinheiro, are you not?

ANTÔNIO

I am and don't you forget it, Seringueiro. Now haven't you some rubber trees to tap?

CHICO

I thought you might need some help.

ANTÔNIO

Help? Why would I need your help? I have everything under control.

CHICO

Doesn't look that way. Didn't sound that way.

ANTÔNIO

Excuse me, excuse me, Seringueiro, but who in the name of São João do you think –?

CHICO removes his seringueiro *hat. ANTÔNIO blanches.*

Chico? (*Terrified.*) We're alright, the villagers, the forest, the farm, we don't want trouble.

CHICO

Who does? But trouble still might find you.

ANTÔNIO

We don't need your kind of trouble, the violence, the shootings. We don't want you, here. No one listens to you anymore. You're not welcome here!

CHICO

But I warned you twenty years ago –

ANTÔNIO

I don't see you. I can't hear you –

CHICO

But can't you hear it on the wind? The rumble. The other villages roundabouts are disappearing. They're coming here. Maybe this year, maybe next. How long do you think you've got?

ANTÔNIO

You're not there!

CHICO

And your people are all disunited –

ANTÔNIO shakes his head to rid himself of the vision.

ANTÔNIO

You're not there. Francisco!

CHICO

And you have a snake in your midst.

Exit ANTÔNIO.

(*Calling after him.*) Beware the anaconda, Antônio, it hugs you, until your spine bursts through your chest. Listen to me, Antônio!

SCENE 3

Enter the WOMEN of the village to mend and wash their quadrilha
dresses on the river bank. CHICO attempts to talk to them.

CHICO

A moment, please, ladies...if you would just stop a moment...
and listen...you must listen to me...please –

CHICO is submerged in the whirl of garments.

FIRST WOMAN

'Mend and wash your dresses, women, or my name's not
Antônio Cícero Machado dos Santos Pinheiro e Pinheiro.'
How are we meant to mend our dresses if we can't buy
anything to mend them with? No wonder the bull won't dance
with us this year.

SECOND WOMAN

Why doesn't the Master lend us the money? He knows how
important it is to us to dance the bull dance each year.

THIRD WOMAN

Because he's as broke as we are.

SECOND WOMAN

But he's the Master.

THIRD WOMAN

He's still broke. Think about it. My husband doesn't catch any
fish. He cannot pay the Master. Your husband can't sell any
beef at market, he can't pay the Master. And so on. He's as
broke as we are.

FIRST WOMAN

So how are we to mend our dresses without buttons and
braiding and bobbins of bright thread?

TIA TEREZA

Use things from the forest. We have shiny stones and brilliant
birds' feathers, and leaves that come in all colours, shapes and
sizes. That's what we used to do in the days before money.

THIRD WOMAN
This is the modern world, Tia Tereza.

SECOND WOMAN
And I so wanted to dance the *quadrilha.*

FIRST WOMAN
Maybe tomorrow we'll get to dance it.

THIRD WOMAN
Only if your Francisco can get the bull to dance first, Catarina.
No *bumba meu boi,* no wedding *quadrilha.*

FIRST WOMAN
And then we'll need a bride and groom.

SECOND WOMAN
I feel young again when I dance the *quadrilha.*

TIA TEREZA
So do I. Especially when I dance it with your husband!

The WOMEN laugh.

CATARINA
Well I'm not looking forward to it. My dress is so faded and
missing so many buttons, it will never be ready for tomorrow
night.

THIRD WOMAN
They fell off last year when you were shaking your hips at
Francisco.

SECOND WOMAN
Chiquinho, Chiquinho, look at my big *bunda.*

CATARINA vomits once again.

FIRST WOMAN
Needs another wash now too.

TIA TEREZA
(*Offering CATARINA some seeds.*) Here, Trininha, take this.

CATARINA
What is it?

TIA TEREZA

Used to eat it in the old days, for morning sickness.

CATARINA

Morning sickness? But I'm not pregnant.

The WOMEN roar with laughter.

SECOND WOMAN

Chiquinho, look at my big *bunda*!

The WOMEN laugh again.

CATARINA

But how did you know? Am I showing already?

*ROSAMARIA creeps out of her front door and around by the trees.
She tries to keep out of CATARINA's eyeline.*

FIRST WOMAN

Where did your Francisco get to when the bull wouldn't
dance, Catarina?

SECOND WOMAN

He needed a rest, she's been working him hard.

THIRD WOMAN

Where is he now?

CATARINA

How should I know where he is, up a *castanheira* tree playing
marbles with a monkey for all I know. I'm not his keeper. (*She
sees ROSAMARIA.*) But I am yours, Rosinha, and I see you. What
are you doing out of the house? Your father said not until you
are married and I didn't notice a line of suitors at our door.

ROSAMARIA

Well I'm going to get myself one.

CATARINA

One what?

ROSAMARIA

One man, one special man.

CATARINA

And where do you plan to get this special man?

ROSAMARIA

Don't know. Down by the river during the Festa.

TIA TEREZA

You'd want to be careful what you might find by the river.

ROSAMARIA

Why's that, Tia Tereza?

TIA TEREZA

The river is full of strange beasts –

THIRD WOMAN

Like the *Cobra Grande*, the giant snake.

ROSAMARIA

What's it like?

SECOND WOMAN

It's wide as the river and longer than the road to town.

THIRD WOMAN

And she rears up from the water, and snatches you from behind!

FIRST WOMAN

She's just a child!

ROSAMARIA

I'm not, I'm a woman.

TIA TEREZA

Or the *Boto*, the pink dolphin that comes ashore in the form of a man –

SECOND WOMAN

Looking for a young woman to be his bride.

ROSAMARIA

And what does he do with them?

TIA TEREZA

Steals them back to the river.

ROSAMARIA

Maybe he'll steal me away so I don't have to spend my days
locked up.

FIRST WOMAN

And live the rest of your life as a fish in the river? Have you
seen the colour of the water recently? And the smell? It smells
as bad as Catarina's dress. All's not well in there.

CATARINA

They're just stories. Old wives' tales. Why don't you help me
for a change? Wring out my dress and hang it on the *Rainha
da Mata*.

ROSAMARIA

Why do they call it the Queen of the Forest?

CATARINA

Because it's been here since before time.

FIRST WOMAN

It was the first tree in the forest, from it all the others come.

THIRD WOMAN

And its fruit, its fruit is the sweetest fruit in the whole of
Amazônia, they say.

ROSAMARIA

Can I taste it?

THIRD WOMAN

It's up so high, look there, at the top, you'd need to find
yourself a brave, brave man to fetch you one.

CATARINA

It makes my tongue taste of honey just to think of it.

FIRST WOMAN

Shouldn't lust after the impossible, Catarina.

TIA TEREZA

Why shouldn't she? It passes the time, before you die!

ROSAMARIA

You look different, Catarina, your body, your cheeks…

The WOMEN laugh. CATARINA continues to eat.

ROSAMARIA

You're pregnant, Catarina! Congratulations! Is Francisco delighted?

CATARINA

If you can find him, you could tell him. No, he'll be terrified when he knows.

ROSAMARIA

But why?

CATARINA

Because he's still a little boy.

ROSAMARIA

At least you've got a man. (*Confidential.*) Come with me tonight.

CATARINA

Where?

ROSAMARIA

To the river.

CATARINA

Why?

ROSAMARIA

Because I was serious, I want to find a man…and I've heard that during the Festa –

CATARINA

Are you crazy? What about your father?

ROSAMARIA

What about him? He's crazy.

CATARINA

Well I'm going crazy stuck in the middle of you two.

ROSAMARIA

Catarina, you're my best friend.

CATARINA

And he's my employer, and the Master of the village.

ROSAMARIA

He hasn't paid you for months.

CATARINA

If I went with you he'd never pay me or Francisco, and there's no other work around. And now we'll have three mouths to feed. (*Eating.*) No way José, it's too dangerous.

ROSAMARIA

But with you there it would be safe –

CATARINA

No.

ROSAMARIA

As my servant, I order you.

CATARINA

I thought I was your best friend.

ROSAMARIA

You are my servant too.

CATARINA

I cannot be both.

CATARINA, furious, gathers her things.

Get back to the house!

ROSAMARIA

I'll be back by dinner.

CATARINA

Now, I order you.

ROSAMARIA

I don't take orders from a servant, I give them. You go back to the house. You prepare dinner, I'm staying by the river, so I can savour the smell of freedom, so I can listen for my man on the wind. I'll be back when the evening bell calls the men from the fields.

Stand off. Eventually CATARINA, impotent, storms off.

And we're to have no more bull dance, I'm going to the river after dinner to find myself a man!

CATARINA

We'll see about that, *menina!*

Exit CATARINA. TIA TEREZA has gathered her things. She beckons ROSAMARIA over.

TIA TEREZA

So it's a man you want, Rosamaria? A special man?

ROSAMARIA

Yes, Tia Tereza.

TIA TEREZA

How much do you want him?

ROSAMARIA

More than anything.

TIA TEREZA

More than anything? In that case, I'll tell you how to get yourself a man, a man for whom you'd be prepared to give up anything. Give me your arm, child. There's a rhyme all the village girls learn when they are young…

> On the rock in the river,
> At half past midnight,
> Three times the lines deliver
> For true love to come to light.

ROSAMARIA

And what are the lines, Tia Tereza, what are the lines I must say three times?

TIA TEREZA

Come with me and I will teach you.

Exit TIA TEREZA and ROSAMARIA.

RICARDO shoulders his saddle.

SCENE 4

Enter FRANCISCO with the BULL.

FRANCISCO

(*Sung.*) Sun's going to shine,
Seed's gonna grow,
Why all these people
Rush to and fro?
Why not have fun,
Lay in the sun?
Like I do, oh I do,
I don't know…

There, *boi*, easy now. Lie down. Relax. That's it. Don't know what got into you there, but no worries now. Just take it easy. Just a few bars of your favourite song and you'll be right as…

ANTÔNIO

(*Off.*) Where is that damned rascal Francisco?

The BULL reacts wildly.

FRANCISCO

(*Sung.*) Sun's gonna shine,
Seed's gonna grow,
Why all these people
Rush to and fro?
Why not have fun,
Play in the sun
Like I do, oh I do, why don't you, me and you, you and
me… (*Whistles.*)

ANTÔNIO

(*Off.*) Francisco!

The BULL reacts wildly.

FRANCISCO

What's wrong with you? It's the Sâo Joâo. Lighten up. Why the long face? How about one of my jokes? There's this *gaucho* from Argentina, that's what they call their cowboys, and he meets this *vaqueiro*, one of our cowboys from Brazil, and he says to the *vaqueiro*, 'In Argentina we're real men, we're all men, we're one hundred per cent men'. And the *vaqueiro* says, 'In Brazil we're about half men and half women, we prefer it that way'.

FRANCISCO laughs. The BULL still distressed but lying down.

What do you call two Argentinian firemen? José and Hose B. Sorry, an old one and a tired one (*Yawns.*) All these jokes have tired me out. How about we get forty winks and then you'll be ready for that dancing. Now just lie there...let me get comfortable and we'll be up and jigging in no time. Can't let me down you know...they'll all pull me apart if you don't dance this year... (*The bull sees CHICO and reacts wildly.*) Woa! What's the matter! There's nothing there. Calm down. (*CHICO calms the bull down.*) That's better. Now let's just get some sleep and then we can think about that dancing...ow! (*Not seeing CHICO, to audience member.*) Who threw that? Did you throw that? You did. You look like just that kind of person who'd –

CHICO hits FRANCISCO from the opposite direction with a book. FRANCISCO marches to other side of stage.

Now I know that was you. I saw you. So you'd better not do it again, because I'll get really, really angry and you wouldn't like me when I'm angry –

CHICO throws another book at him from first direction.

Who did that? Who did that? (*To audience member.*) Look I warned you, I warned you if you did it again I'd have to... well, you know, get really really angry. And now I'm really angry so...so...so just watch it, Buster!

CHICO

Francisco?

FRANCISCO turns to second audience member.

FRANCISCO

You talking to me? Are you talking to me?

CHICO

Francisco.

FRANCISCO

No, you're talking to me.

CHICO

O Francisco!

FRANCISCO

So who is talking to me?

Audience directs him to CHICO.

You? You were talking to me?

CHICO

I was.

FRANCISCO

Do I know you?

CHICO

I'm Chico.

FRANCISCO

Chico who? You're not from round here.

CHICO

I'm from roundabouts.

FRANCISCO

Well Chico Roundabouts, what do you want? We're busy, me and my bull.

CHICO

Busy? No *bumba meu boi* at the Festa Sâo Joâo and now you're just sleeping. Wake up Francisco. There's a lot to be done.

FRANCISCO

My *boi* will dance when it feels like it, won't you *boi*? He takes after me. Now if you don't mind…

CHICO

It's not just the bull, Francisco. There's more going on. Look around you. Listen. Can't you hear them on the wind? Don't you know what's going on in the world?

FRANCISCO

Yes I do. Sun's shining, plants are growing, nature is taking its natural course, and I want to catch some zeds in her fruitilicious bosom, that's what's going on.

CHICO

If you really knew what was going on, you wouldn't be able to sleep.

FRANCISCO

Good thing I don't know then, isn't it, my friend?

FRANCISCO laughs. CHICO hits FRANCISCO with a book.

Ow. (*To CHICO.*) What was that for?

CHICO

It was to make you stop and think.

FRANCISCO

Who says I don't think?

CHICO

About the world.

FRANCISCO

I think about the world. I think about the birds and the fish and the flowers –

CHICO

And what about politics?

FRANCISCO

Boring! I know what I need to know about the world, like if my Master is shouting 'Francisco! Francisco!' I know where I've got to be. Some place else. And I know what I don't need to know, which is everything else.

CHICO

But everything else affects you.

FRANCISCO

Sure it affects me, but I can't affect it, so what's the point in worrying about it?

CHICO

Of course you can't affect it if you don't know about it.

FRANCISCO

Who says I don't know about it? Okay, okay, I'll tell you one about politics, Chico Roundabouts, since you like politics so much: Dick Cheney, The Ex-Vice President of the US of A, says to George W Bush, the The Ex-President of the US of A, he says 'Hey George, did you hear the news?' 'What?' says George. 'Three Brazilian soldiers were shot dead last night.' 'That's terrible,' says George, 'How many is there in a Bra*zillion*?'

FRANCISCO laughs. CHICO hits him with book again.

Double ow! You need to relax, friend, take a leaf out of my book.

CHICO

Do you not care about society? About other people?

FRANCISCO

I do care. I care about Trina, I care that we've got enough.

CHICO

And do you?

FRANCISCO

We get by. Nearly. Not really. No.

CHICO

Why? (*Beat.*) Well?

FRANCISCO

Well it's all the problems in the world, the Master says, isn't it?

CHICO

What problems?

FRANCISCO

The problems; the roads, the trees, the price of beef.
Everything else.

CHICO

Everything else? That's what you call politics, Francisco.

FRANCISCO

It is? You see then, I do know about politics. So I can go back
to sleep.

CHICO

No, Francisco, you've must wake up.

CHICO drops a third book on him.

FRANCISCO

Double, triple ow! What is it with you and these books?

CHICO

You need to look at these.

FRANCISCO

How's a book or a newspaper going to feed me or my family?

CHICO

What's it made from?

FRANCISCO

Paper.

CHICO

And where does paper come from?

FRANCISCO

Trees.

CHICO

And where do trees come from?

FRANCISCO

I see where you're going.

CHICO

Well if you can see where we're going, look in that direction,
rather than behind you.

FRANCISCO

Books are made of paper, paper comes from trees, and cutting down trees is bad, so books are bad and I'm going to sleep.

CHICO

There's no time to sleep! The bull has to dance Francisco. Your village needs you. And this tree you love to sleep under, do you think it will be here for ever? What will you do when you have nowhere to hide from Catarina? You need to do something Francisco, and the first thing you need to do is to pay attention.

FRANCISCO

That's what my teacher always used to say.

CHICO

And what did you say?

FRANCISCO

I'd say I come from a poor family, I can't pay any more.

CHICO

The poor always pay more, Francisco.

FRANCISCO

Same old, same old.

CHICO

Nothing stays the same, Francisco, Look at the seed, look at the flower, look at the fruit in the tree. It's nature's way, it's man's way too. The only way people can deal with change is to work together. And you need to get up off your big fat *bunda* and do something before something is done to you

Enter CATARINA.

FRANCISCO

Nothing's going to change in my world, my friend –

CATARINA

Francisco I've something to tell you.

FRANCISCO

Catarina, my prickly pear!

CATARINA

What were you doing?

FRANCISCO

Working. (*Beat.*) Talking. To Chico.

CATARINA

Chico?

FRANCISCO

My friend. Chico, my wife Catarina, Catarina my friend –

CATARINA

Your friend?

FRANCISCO

Yes. (*To CHICO.*) I'm sorry, my wife, she's been acting funny recently –

CATARINA

Aren't you a bit old for friends like that?

FRANCISCO

Though she's not usually this rude. Catarina, please, don't embarrass me –

CATARINA gestures that FRANCISCO is mad. FRANCISCO turns and gestures to CHICO that CATARINA is mad, but CHICO is gone.

CATARINA

Who's embarrassing who now?

FRANCISCO

But he was here, where's he gone? (*Changing tack.*) So what were you doing for that matter?

CATARINA

What do you think I've been doing? (*Dumps basket of washing. Sighing.*) That Rosamaria, makes me almost as mad as you. I've a good mind to go to her father and…

FRANCISCO

Don't get involved, Trina. He's the Master, and we work for him. Let's keep the relationship professional!

Off we hear ANTÓNIO shout 'Francisco!'

CATARINA

Well some professional you are.

FRANCISCO

I am? Why's that?

CATARINA

You were there. The bull, it didn't dance. The whole village has taken it as a bad sign. The Master's on the war path.

FRANCISCO

(*Going to exit.*) In that case, I'd better go…and see a man about a dog.

CATARINA

Not so fast, I've something to tell you I said…

FRANCISCO

Can't it wait?

CATARINA

No it can't.

FRANCISCO

Why not?

CATARINA

Because I'm… I'm, you know, Francisco…

FRANCISCO

What?

CATARINA

You know!

FRANCISCO

I do?

CATARINA

Yes. I'm pregnant!!!!

FRANCISCO

You mean?

CATARINA

Yes…

FRANCISCO

You're pregnant?

CATARINA

Yes!

FRANCISCO

Like with a baby?

CATARINA

No, with a *macaco* monkey, what do you think, *bobo*?

FRANCISCO

I think…well… I mean wow!… I mean…we should celebrate, shouldn't we?

CATARINA

Yes. With some fruit!

FRANCISCO

Fruit? A good healthy celebration. I've got some fruit. Here, my prickly pear, have a banana.

CATARINA

Have a banana? I'm not having a banana, I'm having your baby, Francisco, I don't want any old fruit, I want a special fruit, a super fruit, a splendicious fruit, I want the fruit from the *Rainha da Mata*.

FRANCISCO

The Queen of the Forest? But that's…

CATARINA

That's what I want.

FRANCISCO

It's bad luck.

CATARINA

I want it, I need it. For the baby, Francisco.

FRANCISCO

But I'd have to climb all the way up −

CATARINA

So?

FRANCISCO

Wait a week or two and it will have fallen down.

CATARINA

And be all bruised and soft? I want it and I want it now! Fetch me the fruit Francisco.

FRANCISCO

Or?

CATARINA

There is no 'or', Francisco.

Beat. FRANCISCO knows she's serious.

FRANCISCO

Of course, Catarina, of course, my prickly *piranha*.

Duet.

CATARINA

It's time, my dear,
Become a man,
Get up the tree,
Bring down the fruit for me.
Go up, my dear,
Do what you can
For your family,
Take responsibility.

FRANCISCO

Are you going out of your mind,
Darling pregnant wife of mine?
With a baby now inside,
You've gone insane!

I can never go that high,
Just as hard as I may try.
I will do it, please don't cry,
But you're insane!

CATARINA

Higher, husband! Higher, husband –

CATARINA / FRANCISCO

Further to the top / No way to the top –

CATARINA

Stretch a little higher,
Fetch the fruit –

CATARINA / FRANCISCO

And let it drop / I'm gonna drop –

CATARINA

Higher husband, higher husband –

CATARINA / FRANCISCO

Put your legs to use / My legs are of no use –
Bring me down the fruit / But I'll bring you down the
  fruit –
And let me suck upon its juice / And let you suck upon
  its juice.

*FRANCISCO has retrieved the fruit. He drops it down to CATARINA
and descends while CATARINA greedily eats the fruit.*

FRANCISCO

So for once, wife of mine, are you satisfied with what
  I've done?

CATARINA

(*Greedily eating.*) Yes, Chiquinho, yes I am satisfied.
(*Kisses him.*) Now fetch me another one.

The village bells rings.

Damn it, the Master's dinner.

FRANCISCO

That's what you call saved by the bell.

SCENE 5

Bell continues to ring. CATARINA enters with a team of servants and arranges dinner for the Master's family.

>   CATARINA
> (*Singing.*) *Camu-camu e caju*
> *Tamarindo, cupuaçu.*
> Let's sing the forest,
> Let's sing its fruits.
>
> *Camu-camu e caju,*
> *Tamarindo, cupuaçu.*
> That's two for me
> And one for you.

>   TIA TEREZA
> *Pato e caruru,*
> *Piranha e pirarucu.*
> Let's sing the river,
> Let's sing its food.

>   CATARINA / TIA TEREZA
> *Pato e caruru,*
> *Piranha e pirarucu.*
> What is in the river?
> I'll eat it too.

>   TIA TEREZA
> *Açaí na tigela –*

>   CATARINA
> *Banana com sorvete –*

>   TIA TEREZA / CATARINA
> *Mangaba,* our food is tropical –

>   TIA TEREZA
> *Pirão de aipim –*

>   CATARINA
> *Macaco tucupi –*

> TIA TEREZA / CATARINA

From the forest Amazônia has it all!

> ALL

Camu-camu –

> CATARINA

Bodó Juriti –

> ALL

Camu-camu –

> TIA TEREZA

Jaca sapoti –

> ALL

Camu-camu –

> CATARINA

Goiaba buriti –

> ALL

Camu-camu –

> TIA TEREZA / CATARINA

Mari-mari.

Enter RICARDO. He is covered in mud and dung.

> RICARDO

What's for dinner?

> CATARINA

Forest fruit, wild piglet, duck, monkey, catfish, electric eel –

> RICARDO

(*Bored.*) The usual. I'd kill for a McDonalds.

> CATARINA

(*Catching the smell.*) What happened to you, Ricardo? Have you had a little accident?

> RICARDO

Yes, I've had an accident! I was herding cattle by the river on horseback, a heifer bolted for the trees, I went after it, and a branch knocked me out of my saddle.

> CATARINA

And into a mound of monkey *merda*!

> RICARDO

It was the trees. If it wasn't for them, we could herd the cattle in pick-ups or four-by-fours.

CATARINA helps him remove his clothes and into a tin bath.

> RICARDO

You know rich mothers in the city, I'd see them when I was walking to University, they drive their kids to school in four-by-fours. And Uncle wonders why we can't make any money? If only he trusted me, if only he gave me a chance. I'd show him what I learnt at University. I'd show him what could be done with this place –

> CATARINA

Well you're not the Master.

> RICARDO

No. No I am not. And where is the Master, my Uncle?

> ANTÔNIO

(*Off.*) Francisco where in damnation…

> CATARINA

With his bull, looking for his *pião*, my husband, by the sound of it.

Enter ROSAMARIA from upstairs.

> RICARDO

He actually thinks a dancing bull will save the farm?

> CATARINA

No, he believes São João will save the farm if the bull dances. It's the dancing keeps us strong. It's our tradition.

> RICARDO

Tradition is what is left for the tourists, when we are finally forced give up farming.

RICARDO, semi-naked, draws himself up when he sees ROSAMARIA.

ROSAMARIA

Is that you, Cousin Ricardo?

RICARDO

Yes, it's me, Rosa.

ROSAMARIA

I meant the smell, Cousin Ricardo, the smell of shit, is that you?

RICARDO

I have been working on my Uncle's farm, Cousin Rosamaria.

ROSAMARIA

I wish I was allowed to work on my father's farm, Cousin Ricardo. I wouldn't even mind smelling as bad as you do. Though I do appear to have got some mud upon my skirt.(*To CATARINA pointedly.*) Housekeeper, I appear to have got some mud upon my skirt.

CATARINA

That is most strange, *senhorita*, since you were confined to the house today.

ROSAMARIA

Indeed it is. Perhaps the house is not as clean as it should be, Dona Catarina, since I was confined to the house and I have, nevertheless, managed to get mud upon my skirt.

CATARINA

(*Eating.*) There again, perhaps it not the house that needs a good cleaning, *senhorita*, but your dirty mind.

ROSAMARIA

Neither you, nor my father, will brainwash me, Dona Catarina. But I still wish to wash my exterior, so draw me fresh water.

CATARINA

I'm afraid that that in which the young master is bathing himself is all that I've managed to draw up from the river in my condition. So tough tamarind, you'll have to share with him.

ROSAMARIA

The young master! Who could that be?

CATARINA smiles. She removes RICARDO's clothes to one side and goes to fetch RICARDO fresh clothes. ROSAMARIA washes alongside RICARDO.

RICARDO

At University, in the city, we had our own rooms, with showers and hot running water and even air-conditioning.

ROSAMARIA does not respond.

I had a television too. Fifty channels.

ROSAMARIA does not respond.

And there were bars and discos. I'd go there in the evenings and meet girls –

ROSAMARIA

In your dreams.

RICARDO

I'd lots of girlfriends.

ROSAMARIA

O yes? Where are they? If everything was so wonderful at University, in the city, why didn't you stay?

RICARDO

Because I wanted to come back, to help Uncle. He paid for my education, he should reap some of the benefits.

ROSAMARIA

How very generous of you.

Pause.

RICARDO

I saw you earlier, down by the river.

ROSAMARIA

You were spying on me?

RICARDO

No.

ROSAMARIA

Do you like to spy on me, Cousin Ricardo? Do you like to
look at me? I would have thought at the University, in the city,
the 'beautiful girls' in the discos and the bars would have been
much more…worthy of your attentions. (*Beat.*) So is there
something that pleases you about our little farm after all?

RICARDO

No. Don't be sick! And I've never said I don't like this farm –

ROSAMARIA

No, but you think us stupid peasants.

RICARDO

I've never said that –

ROSAMARIA

'But Uncle, in the University this, in the University that…' –

RICARDO

I love my uncle.

ROSAMARIA

Bunda licker. I hate my father.

RICARDO

I love my uncle.

ROSAMARIA

You're jealous of me, that I'm his child.

RICARDO

I'm not.

ROSAMARIA

Even though it's you who got the education and me who's
locked up in the house.

RICARDO

You weren't locked up. I saw you, I said. I know what you're
planning tonight.

ROSAMARIA

And what are you planning to do about it?

Enter ANTÔNIO.

ANTÔNIO

Where is that infernal Francisco?

RICARDO

Good evening, Uncle Antônio.

ANTÔNIO

And what is that awful smell?

ROSAMARIA

It's Ricardo, father, he stinks.

ANTÔNIO

Catarina, where in damnation is Francisco? I've been looking for him high and low.

CATARINA

He had to see a man about some dog.

ANTÔNIO

Well tell him he has to see his Master about a bull and that if he isn't here faster than I can say Antônio Cícero Machado dos Santos Pinheiro e Pinheiro, he will find himself trussed and roasted and on my plate with the pig, the eel and the monkey!

CATARINA

Yes, Seu Antônio.

Exit CATARINA.

RICARDO

I put the cattle in the river field, Uncle Antônio.

ANTÔNIO

Thank you, Ricardo.

RICARDO

I repaired the fencing too.

ANTÔNIO

You're a good nephew.

Pause.

RICARDO

Rosamaria was out by the river today too.

ANTÔNIO

What?

RICARDO

With the women, mending the dresses –

ANTÔNIO

But I distinctly ordered Catarina that until I find her a husband –

RICARDO

Then she went off with that *bruxa* Tia Tereza.

ANTÔNIO

What do you have to say about this, Rosamaria?

ROSAMARIA

If you didn't lock me up, you wouldn't have a problem with me escaping.

ANTÔNIO

No, no, if I locked you up properly then I wouldn't have this problem at all.

RICARDO

And I heard her, she's planning to return there tonight. And it's a full moon and the *Festa de São João.*

ANTÔNIO

She is, is she? Well we'll see about that. Catarina!

Enter CATARINA with FRANCISCO. He carries a book.

CATARINA

I found him Seu Antônio.

FRANCISCO

You were looking for me Seu?

ANTÔNIO

(*Fuming.*) Francisco! You, you, you…! Where have you been you good for nothing?

FRANCISCO

I was looking at a book.

ANTÔNIO

A book? Since when does my *pião* need books?

FRANCISCO

That does not show a commitment to staff development, Seu Antônio.

ANTÔNIO

I don't want my staff to develop, I want my bull to dance.

FRANCISCO

I just need a bit more time with him, Seu Antônio. I've sung him his favourite song and told him my best jokes…he's not dancing yet, but give it time…

ANTÔNIO

Jokes? Do you think this is funny?

FRANCISCO

No, and nor did he. That's the problem. He's just lying there, but I'll get some better jokes and sing him some more songs and he'll soon be dancing for me again.

ANTÔNIO

For you perhaps, but not for São João. For São João he ran wild, crazy, amok. It's a sign, a bad sign. And now Rosamaria is running amok too. For us to survive and thrive again, the bull must dance, and as the Master I must ensure that he does. That's why I must go to town. I'll buy a golden new crown for the bull.

ROSAMARIA

But what with?

ANTÔNIO

Credit. The name of Antônio Cícero Machado dos Santos Pinheiro e Pinheiro is still good in these parts. And while I'm there I'll find a husband for you. A man of substance.

ROSAMARIA

But Father –

RICARDO

And let me look after the farm while you're gone, Uncle?

ROSAMARIA

I'm not going to marry just anyone –

RICARDO

And the bull and Rosamaria?

ROSAMARIA

No father, please –

FRANCISCO

No, Seu Antônio, I beg you too, he doesn't understand the bull.

ROSAMARIA

Nor women.

RICARDO

I see no woman.

ROSAMARIA

Nor anything.

ANTÔNIO

Enough. Know that I, Antônio Cícero Machado dos Santos Pinheiro e Pinheiro, in my temporary absence, divide in three my little kingdom. Ricardo you shall look after the farm. Catarina, you shall look after Rosamaria. Since she so easily escaped the house, you shall lock her in her room and guard her closely. And Francisco, you shall look after the bull. And if he does not dance tomorrow night, we shall all watch you dance barefoot on hot coals.

RICARDO

While I whip your feet, *pião*.

ANTÔNIO

So Francisco, out to the field with you. You and my bull shall dance all night if you have to, but you shall get it right tomorrow.

Exit FRANCISCO and BULL.

Now, my horse, my horse, I've settled my three kingdoms, I just need a horse. I must set off straight away if I'm to make town by dawn and return for the *bumba meu boi* tomorrow night.

    ANTÔNIO's horse is brought in.

VILLAGERS

    He's off to town
    To buy the crown,
    Upon his horse,
    He shall not alter course.

    He shall return,
    He'll not his people spurn,
    He's now on course,
    Our Master on his horse.

    Then for São João,
    The golden crown
    On the bull's brow.
    Come now and pray
    For our last only chance.
    Once again the bull shall dance.

ANTÔNIO / VILLAGERS

I'm off to town / he's off to town –
To buy the bull a crown / ….a crown –
Upon my horse / Upon his horse –
I shall not alter course / course –
I shall return / He shall return –
I'll not my people spurn / spurn –
The crown I'll bring / The crown he'll bring –
To make our bull our king / our king.

ALL

    Then for São João –
    The golden crown
    On the bull's brow,
    Come now and pray
    For our last and only chance.
    Once again the bull shall dance.

Exit ANTÔNIO. Exit RICARDO in opposite direction.

CATARINA

And you, *senhorita*, to your room –

ROSAMARIA turns towards room, stops. She picks up RICARDO's dirty clothes. CATARINA does not see, she is eating. Exit ROSAMARIA to bedroom.

CATARINA

(*Spitting out food disgusted.*) What is wrong with me? Whatever I eat is not enough. I want something, something more delicate, something more delectable, something more delicious. What is it I want?…it's on the tip of my tongue… I want… I want –

It suddenly strikes CATARINA what she wants. She rushes to find FRANCISCO.

Francisco! Francisco!

Exit CATARINA.

SCENE 6

Enter BULL. FRANCISCO follows, clinging on to rope.

FRANCISCO

Slow down *boi*, slow down you boneheaded bull. Why are you
leading me such a merry dance so deep into the forest?

*FRANCISCO has caught up with the BULL. FRANCISCO calms
him and ties him to a tree.*

What's got into you my beauty? Will you still not dance the
bumba? Won't you even dance for your Daddy? For old Pai
Francisco? That means Daddy Francisco. That's right, *boi*, I've
been so busy chasing after you, I haven't even had time to
tell you, that I'm going to be a Daddy. I'll father a whole herd
like you, and like you I'll bulldoze my way through the forest
snorting 'Out of my way – don't you know who I am? I'm Pai
Francisco.'

*FRANCISCO has been slowly starting to dance. The BULL starts
dancing too.*

That's it, *boi*. You remember how to shake those hips? You
remember your smooth moves –

The BULL startles and strains at the tether.

No *boi*, woa there *boi*! What's wrong with you? You look
frightened. (*Seeing CHICO.*) Chico? Chico Roundabouts can
you help me?

CHICO

Now you want my help.

FRANCISCO

There's something wrong with him, he's not himself.

CHICO

You wait a few weeks and he'll sort himself out on his own.

FRANCISCO

But the master says he must dance by tomorrow night.

CHICO

I'm just taking a leaf out of your book, Francisco. Why do you think he's scared?

FRANCISCO

I don't know. It's hard to think when you've got a raging bull on your hands.

CHICO

First you were too lazy to think, now you're too busy. Always some excuse.

CHICO whispers to the BULL and calms him.

How do you know a thunderstorm is on the way? Because the birds take flight in the opposite direction and the monkeys go silent in the trees.

FRANCISCO

What's this got to do with monkeys and birds?

CHICO

Because animals are smarter than us, they sense danger long before humans. Why is he angry and scared?

FRANCISCO

Because he senses something?

CHICO

Good.

FRANCISCO

What?

CHICO

Think, won't you? Trouble of course.

FRANCISCO

What kind of trouble?

CHICO

The kind that would frighten him so much that he'd run from his field and into the forest for shelter. He senses destruction.

FRANCISCO

But what can I do about that? I just have to make him dance.
If I don't make him dance, they're going to make me dance on
hot coals and whip my feet.

CHICO

Always thinking of yourself. It's not just about making him
dance.

FRANCISCO

It is to me.

CHICO

The bull is connected to the forest. He senses the coming
destruction. You must put right the reasons or he'll never
dance for São João. You must bring your community together
to defend itself and the forest.

FRANCISCO

Me? Bring the community together? That's the Master's job,
mine is to make the bull dance.

CHICO

But you're the only one who'll listen to me, so it's got to be
you, whether you or I like it or not.

FRANCISCO

But I can't lead anyone, I can't even get my own wife to do
anything I want. I don't understand, Chico.

CHICO

Everyone's acting on their own. Thinking of themselves. Why
there's no fish or why they can't sell their beef. No one is
thinking of the whole picture. The forest and the people. Look,
look at this stick.

CHICO snaps it.

One stick on its own, easy to break, but a bunch of sticks –

CHICO cannot break it.

The bunch is much stronger than the single one. One stick is
the single person on their own. The bunch is the community,

stronger together. You must persuade everyone to act as a community together.

FRANCISCO

This might be of help if I had to teach a stick to dance, but I've to teach a bull. Sticks! Look, I'm busy, I'm busy. I'm not a leader, I'm a simple *pião*, a farmhand, friend, and I've got work to do.

CHICO

But you're the only one who listens to me. You must listen to me.

FRANCISCO

I'm not listening to you, I'm trying to get my bull to dance.

The BULL goes wild. CHICO unties the BULL. The BULL exits with FRANCISCO trailing behind him.

Slow down *boi*, slow down you boneheaded bull. Chico!

The BULL takes off again, dragging FRANCISCO after it.

SCENE 7

The forest.

TIA TEREZA

(*Sings.*) Moon shines in the dark,
Fish teem down the river,
Play and dance all night long,
Entranced by the moonlight's song.

She hears in the dark,
'Be my love for ever'.
Will this girl be strong,
Bewitched by the moonlight's song?

She knows in her heart
This night is forever.
Because she's the one,
Beloved by the moonlight's song.

Enter a boy. He has run away from home. When he is sure that he is unobserved he takes off his hat and reveals that he is ROSAMARIA dressed in RICARDO's clothes.

ROSAMARIA

(*She smells the suit.*) I might smell like a baboon's *bunda*, but at least I'm free. (*She laughs.*) Dressed like this I feel I could climb down from the highest window, shin down twenty drainpipes and run through twenty times twenty fields. Catarina was too busy looking for something more to eat to see me slipping off and Ricardo just took me for another of the village men when I passed them by. Who would have thought freedom would smell so bad and be so good? (*She looks around.*) Now, what was this that Tia Tereza said?

(*From memory.*) On the rock in the river,
At half past midnight,
Three times the lines deliver
For your love to come to light.

The rock in the river…

ROSAMARIA looks around for the correct rock. She finds it.

At half past midnight –

ROSAMARIA checks her watch. She has enough time. She quickly removes RICARDO's clothes. She looks at her watch again. She counts down five seconds.

Three times the lines deliver,
For your love to come to light –
(*Nervously.*) Come changeling of the wild –

She looks around. Perhaps it was an animal.

Come changeling of the wild,
Come claim your nature's child.

She looks around...nothing.

Come changeling of the wild,
Come claim your nature's child.

She waits, trembling. Nothing. And again nothing. She sits up. Nothing. She decides nothing is going to happen. She shivers, she is cold. She puts on RICARDO's clothes once more. Thoroughly disheartened she is about to leave when the BOTO appears with a mighty rush from the water.

He sweeps her off her feet.

SCENE 8

RICARDO addresses the workers of the village. CHICO watches from the audience.

RICARDO
My friends, fellow Amazônians, villagers, I wish to help you not to hinder you. I make no claim to be an expert, like the rest of you, in the arts of farming. No cowboy like you, Seu Vaqueiro, who understands the very minds of beasts and how best to raise and herd and slaughter them. Nor fisherman, like you Seu Pescador, who can trace the ten thousand waterways of ten times ten thousand fish, nor am I an expert rubber-tapper who, like you Senhorita Seringueira, can map every rubber tree and every other tree besides for ten miles around. I am but a humble student recently returned from the University. So you tell me, Seu Vaqueiro, why have you no money?

VAQUEIRO
Because we have so few cattle and so little space to feed them.

RICARDO
And you, Seu Pescador, why have you no money?

PESCADOR
Because the water in the river has changed, the fish are dying.

RICARDO
And you Senhorita Seringueira, why have you no money?

SERINGUEIRA
Because they come into the forest at night to cut down trees.

RICARDO
Do you think a dancing bull will stop people polluting the river? Do you think a dancing bull will stop the illegal loggers? Every year you dance the bull dance because things are bad, and every year things get worse. Do you think Sâo Joâo is listening to you anymore? You must learn to help yourselves. Because otherwise, someone else will help themselves to everything we have here. If we don't start to make money out

of our land there are plenty of others who will. Seu Vaqueiro would you like money?

VAQUEIRO

Yes…

RICARDO

Seu Pescador? Senhorita Seringueira?

PESCADOR

Of course.

SERINGUEIRA

Who wouldn't?

RICARDO

Well, I might not have learned how to farm or fish or tap rubber trees, but I learned how money is made out of the land. I learned about economics. The days of the small farm are finished, as are the days of the *seringueiro* and the small fishermen. It's not one magic bull and a hundred cattle that you need, but one hard working bull and a thousand cattle with enough land to graze upon and grow fat upon. Then we too would have a big *fazenda*.

VAQUEIRO

But how will you make a big *fazenda* out of this little farm?

RICARDO

By cutting down the trees. Listen to me, my friends. This very night. We will work all night, and cut down every tree in the Master's forest. What we don't cut down we'll burn. The ash will fertilise the land. And out of that ash shall rise a modern *fazenda*. You won't have to walk your endless rubber route, Senhorita Seringueira.

CHICO

But that is your life, Senhorita Seringueira.

SERINGUEIRA

But that is my life, Ricardo.

RICARDO

That hard life is over. Nor will you have to rely on a polluted river, Seu Pescador.

CHICO

But you have worked the river since you were a boy.

PESCADOR

But I have worked on the water since I was a small boy.

RICARDO

In poverty. Why should we not be allowed to live as the rest of the world does? Just because we live in Amazônia, the rest of the world expects us to live in simple poverty. Why shouldn't we have roads and air-conditioning and airports? The rest of the world have them and yet they tell us that we can't? They have chopped down their trees so that they can have houses, cars, buses, football pitches, cinemas…why can't we? Why should we live in a different century from the rest of the world? We want order and we want progress – what it says upon our nation's flag. Why shouldn't we have a modern *fazenda*? Herd our cattle in pick-up trucks and four-by-fours. I promise you, in one year's time you will all be rich and we will have the finest bull dance in the region.

VAQUEIRO

Sounds good to me, my horse is old and fit to drop.

CHICO

But the land is nothing without the trees, it's poor, it will wash away into the river –

RICARDO

Who said that? It won't, it won't.

PESCADOR

What?

RICARDO

Why won't you listen? Don't you know about the soil? Don't you know about economics? Listen: I'm the Master for tonight.

VAQUEIRO

But what about when the Master comes back?

RICARDO

He'll be amazed to find his little farm turned into a great *fazenda*.

SERINGUEIRA

But you can't cut down a forest.

RICARDO

Why shouldn't we? All the great countries of the world have done, the United States, Britain, Russia, France, Germany –

CHICO

If America sticks its head into the fire, does that mean we should too?

RICARDO

(*To audience member.*) America is the modern world, it's time we joined the modern world.

VILLAGERS

Yes.

CHICO

But it will destroy this community.

RICARDO

What was that?

CHICO

It was your conscience. It was the truth.

RICARDO

It won't destroy the community

VAQUEIRO

Who said it did, Seu Ricardo?

RICARDO

No one. Do not listen. Here my friends, take these.

RICARDO hands out axes, saws and chainsaws.

CHICO

He's lying when you say they'll all be driving four-by-fours.
He's lying when says you'll all be rich. There won't even be
enough work to go around.

RICARDO

Stop it.

VAQUEIRO

Stop?

RICARDO

No go. Go all of you. Get to work now.

CHICO

No, you can't.

SERINGUEIRA

No, no I can't. Even if I die of hunger.

RICARDO

Look what you've done. Turning us against ourselves. What
are you? Hiding in the shadows. We don't want to live in the
shadows any longer, do we?

VILLAGERS

No.

RICARDO

Then let us cut ourselves a clear view of the sky. And even if
the *seringueiros* are against us, let us *vaqueiros* and *pescadors* stick
together.

They set to work.

CHICO

But the earth, the earth here is not fertile without the trees. In
a few years this land will be a wasteland.

RICARDO

Who are you? Where are you speaking from?

CHICO

Like you said, from the shadows. From the shadows inside
your head.

RICARDO

What's your name troublemaker?

CHICO

I am you. I am all of you.

RICARDO

You are not me. You want this village to rot away and die. The only way they can save themselves is to make the land work for them, not waste their lives scratching a living out of the disappearing forest. They must work with the forces that are coming and save themselves.

CHICO

They must resist the forces that are coming and save us all.

RICARDO

How can you resist the inevitable? Join us. Those who resist will cease to exist.

CHICO

We'll always be here Ricardo.

RICARDO

Just the dying echo of a language no one speaks anymore.

CHICO

Working together we have enough for everybody's needs.

RICARDO

What do you know of economics?

CHICO

I know that if I was on a ship in a storm I would want a sailor who'd sailed safely through stormy seas at the helm, not someone who knew the price of boats. If you want to know about this forest, Seu Ricardo, you don't ask the economists, you ask those who've lived and worked in this forest.

RICARDO

I am and they're saying they're with me.

CHICO

Because you are blinding them with false dreams of wealth. This forest is on fire, you need someone who's been through the fire, who's been buried in the forest itself to show you the way out of the flames.

RICARDO

And you know about being buried in the forest?!

CHICO

What you're doing will be the death of this place, and of the world.

RICARDO

And you know about death do you? You know nothing, how could you? An ignorant peasant, kept in ignorance by those whose interest it is in to keep you so. This is the future of the world.

SCENE 9

Enter CATARINA.

CATARINA

Francisco? Francisco where are you? Why are you taking
the master's bull so deep into the forest? Francisco, there's
something I want, something I need, something you have to
get for me.

*She is tired and noticeably more pregnant. She must sit down
to catch her breath. Perhaps she eats a snack. She gathers her
strength sets off after FRANCISCO.*

*Enter FRANCISCO and the BULL. The BULL stops and will
not move.*

FRANCISCO

(*Wearily.*) First you won't stand still, now you won't move.
What is wrong with you, *boi*? Dance or they'll kill me.
And you don't want me dead? And you and my little baby
Francisco without a Daddy, do you?

CATARINA

So there you are.

FRANCISCO

Trina, what are you doing here? It's late.

CATARINA

Because I'm hungry.

FRANCISCO

But you've eaten –

CATARINA

I'm hungry! I'm hungry!

FRANCISCO

Okay. (*Soothing.*) Okay.

CATARINA

I want some eggs.

FRANCISCO

Eggs? He's a bull not a hen.

CATARINA

Not hen eggs, not bull eggs but snake eggs.

FRANCISCO

Snake eggs?

CATARINA

The black snake eggs of the *Cobra Grande* –

FRANCISCO

The *Cobra Grande*?

CATARINA

Yes.

FRANCISCO

Who lives in the river, and is as wide as the river, and as long as the river?

CATARINA

Yes.

FRANCISCO

No.

CATARINA

Yes.

FRANCISCO

No! If I try to steal its eggs, her little babies she'll –

FRANCISCO mimes what the Cobra Grande *will do to him.*

CATARINA

I want it. I need it. For my little baby Francisco. If you don't do it, I'll –

CATARINA mimes what she will do to him.

FRANCISCO

But I must teach the Master's bull dance by tomorrow or I'm dead –

CATARINA

You'll be dead sooner if you don't get it for me.

FRANCISCO

But Trina –!

CATARINA

Get it for me! Get it for me now!

CATARINA pushes him into the water. There is much thrashing about in the water. We see a giant green tail, an ugly eye, a long serpent's tongue. FRANCISCO comes up for air.

FRANCISCO

Trina, Trina please!

CATARINA

(*Sung.*) Deeper husband, deeper husband,
Down into the water,
Fetch the black eggs below,
And bring it back to feed your daughter.

FRANCISCO sticks his head out of the water.

FRANCISCO

Daughter?
I can never go that deep,
But I'll go beyond my reach,
There is something now in me,
I must be insane.

Your desires have made me wild,
And I'll risk it for our child,
I'll regret it in a while,
I must be insane.

FRANCISCO is dragged back under the water.

CATARINA

Deeper husband, deeper husband,
If you love your daughter,
I want the *Cobra*'s eggs
Deep at the bottom of the water.

FRANCISCO is dragged back under the water.

FRANCISCO

It's got my, the *Cobra Grande*'s got my…!

She pushes him under the water. He bobs up again.

CATARINA

I can taste what the *Cobra* will give to our daughter.
Feed me, Francisco, feed me.

CATARINA pushes him under once more. Long Pause. CATARINA looks at the water. She fears FRANCISCO is dead.

Francisco? Chiquinho?

Enter FRANCISCO from behind her, his clothes shredded, with his hands full of black Cobra Grande eggs. He taps her on the shoulder. She is momentarily delighted to see he is alive, then devours the eggs.

FRANCISCO

Now, you wanted the fruit, I got you the fruit. You wanted the snake eggs, I got you the black snake eggs of the *Cobra Grande*. So, Catarina, my wife, are you satisfied?

CATARINA

(*Greedily eating.*) Yes, Chiquinho, yes I am satisfied.

FRANCISCO

Good.

CATARINA

I do not want any more eggs.

FRANCISCO

Good.

CATARINA

I do not want another fruit from the *Rainha da Mata*.

FRANCISCO

Good. So in that case, I hope you don't mind, but I've got a bull to teach –

CATARINA

All I want, all I want, all I want is….

CATARINA looks to the BULL.

FRANCISCO

No.

CATARINA

Yes.

FRANCISCO

No!

CATARINA

Yes.

FRANCISCO

Not the Master's bull. Not my *boi*!

CATARINA

No. Not all of him. Just his tongue.

FRANCISCO

His tongue?

CATARINA

Yes, his tongue.

FRANCISCO

No, please don't ask me, Trina –

CATARINA

I want his tongue, Francisco, I want the bull's tongue. You'll get me his tongue.

Pause. The BULL bolts once more for the forest as the sound of axes, chainsaws and fire destroying the forest grows louder.

Act Two

The Forest.

CHICO

And the world slept
As our forest was lost,
And the Amazon burned.
It was too late that we learned
Where is the hope,
The belief that there still
Is a way to return?

In the distance the VAQUEIROS sing their cutting chorus.

ROSAMARIA lies asleep alone, dressed in her slip.

ROSAMARIA
(*Waking but still in a dream.*) I never want to leave the forest, I never want to leave you, my love –

ROSAMARIA goes to kiss the BOTO but he is not there. She looks around for him.

My love? My love where are you? My love?!

She hears something.

What's that? (*Looking off.*) My father!

ROSAMARIA dresses in RICARDO's clothes.

Enter ANTÓNIO on horse. He drinks from a bottle. He is drunk. He crashes into a tree.

ANTÓNIO
You there! Young Man! *Jovem!* Would you care to help me with my horse. It's not working properly.

ROSAMARIA brings ANTÓNIO's horse under control.

You're a kind man, *jovem.* You're not from round here are you?

ROSAMARIA

No. I'm from the city. I'm visiting a friend from University.

ANTÔNIO

And this friend lives in Todos Os Santos?

ROSAMARIA

On a farm with his Uncle, Antônio Cícero Machado dos
Santos Pinheiro e Pinheiro.

ANTÔNIO

I am Antônio Cícero Machado dos Santos Pinheiro e Pinheiro.

ROSAMARIA

You are Antônio Cícero Machado dos Santos Pinheiro e
Pinheiro?

ANTÔNIO

The selfsame.

ROSAMARIA

Sir, it is an honour indeed. Ricardo has told me much about
you.

ANTÔNIO

Ah Ricardo's friend? He's a good boy, Ricardo.

ROSAMARIA

Besides general report of your good name reaches even the
city.

ANTÔNIO

It does?

ROSAMARIA

Yes. You're a big name in the city. You're a big name
everywhere!

ANTÔNIO

Well, that is gratifying to know. In the city perhaps a good
name is all one needs. But in the town it is no longer so. I
went to town, to buy my bull a crown, but no one would lend
me money. People just laughed when I asked. One said 'I'll
give you money for the crown, in return for your farm'. And

then another said 'Forget your crown and your bull dance and let me buy the whole village'. And I shouted 'No, Never!' and they laughed louder. Then a third man, a stranger, said 'Forget your farm and village. Me and my bulldozers are coming to build a huge wide road, right through Todos Os Santos.' And he took out papers and deeds and documents that say I don't really own any of this land. That I am master of nothing! My father and my grandfather and grandfather's grandfather have farmed this land, and now some stranger from the town thinks he can just take it from me. They're circling overhead now, all round us, like *urubas*. And it's my carcass they're waiting to feed on. Any moment now they could swoop.

> ROSAMARIA

São João will never let this happen.

> ANTÔNIO

But how can I stop them, *jovem*?

> ROSAMARIA

Don't lose heart, Seu. If you are the same Antônio Cícero Machado dos Santos Pinheiro e Pinheiro, whose name is known far and wide, then you will find a way. You'll make your *boi bumba*, even without a crown, and the blessing of São João will rain down on all the village.

> ANTÔNIO

Young man, you're right. I swore on my name Todos Os Santos would dance the *bumba meu boi* tonight, so dance we will. But there's another problem.

> ROSAMARIA

There is?

> ANTÔNIO

Yes. (*Suddenly gloomy.*) The *quadrilha*. For that dance we need a bride and groom. Not only did I fail to get my bull a crown, I failed to find my daughter a husband too. With my land under threat I couldn't persuade anyone in town to marry her. They laughed at me, and they laughed at her too. My poor, poor Rosamaria. No man of substance will ever want you.

ROSAMARIA

Excuse me Seu Antônio, but isn't your daughter the beautiful
Rosamaria?

ANTÔNIO

She is.

ROSAMARIA

The Rosamaria? The famous Rosamaria who's renowned
throughout the Amazon for her great beauty, her enormous
intelligence, her seductive charm and her hilarious wit?

ANTÔNIO

I think so. But –

ROSAMARIA

The one they call the brightest star in the southern skies? The
sweetest song in the dawn chorus? The reddest orchid in the
heart of the forest?

ANTÔNIO

That's her but –

ROSAMARIA

The Rosamaria who is the most desirable woman in all of
Brazil? Surely, Seu Antônio, you will have no trouble finding a
husband for her.

Beat.

ANTÔNIO

What's your name *jovem*?

ROSAMARIA

My name is Silvio, Seu Antônio.

ANTÔNIO

I like you *jovem*, you have a certain air.

ROSAMARIA

I had a little accident.

ANTÔNIO

Oh well. As the saying goes, a big smell does not mean a small
soul. Perhaps you'd care to accompany me to Todos Os Santos

tonight. There you will be my guest at the Festa São João. You will watch my *boi* dance the *bumba*, crown or no crown. And after that, Senhor, you will dance the wedding *quadrilha* with the brightest star, the sweetest song, the reddest orchid. That's right, my daughter, Rosamaria!

ROSAMARIA

Me? Dance the *quadrilha*?

ANTÔNIO

Yes.

ROSAMARIA

With your daughter?

ANTÔNIO

Yes.

ROSAMARIA

Ah. But *senhor*, I am not worthy of such a woman.

ANTÔNIO

Yes you are.

ROSAMARIA

No I'm not. Believe me, she is so much better a woman than I am a man.

ANTÔNIO

Silvio, your modesty is proof of your great worth. You are truly a fitting match for my Rosa, and I insist.

ROSAMARIA

Senhor, I am afraid you have forced me to reveal, truthfully, why I cannot marry your daughter.

ANTÔNIO

And why is that, *senhor*?

ROSAMARIA

Because, because truthfully I am not attracted to women.

ANTÔNIO

You're not?

ROSAMARIA

No.

ANTÔNIO

O. That's…that's…you know… I mean we're very open minded here, in my village… But are you sure?

ROSAMARIA

Yes, absolutely sure, Seu. However, I do know a man, a friend, a close friend, who is the perfect match for your daughter.

ANTÔNIO

You do? Is he a man of substance like you Silvio?

ROSAMARIO

Oh, he's got substance alright! Lots of it! Tonight, when the bull dances its *bumba*, I will bring this man to the Todos Os Santos, and he will partner your daughter in the wedding *quadrilha*! But only if it pleases you, Seu…

ANTÔNIO

Silvio, I trust your judgement totally. It's strange, it's as though I've known you all my life.

ROSAMARIA

That settles it. You bring the *boi*, I'll bring the man.

ANTÔNIO

Jovem, it's a deal!

They go to exit in opposite directions. Enter CHICO.

CHICO

Seu Antônio, you must come –

ANTÔNIO

You again –

ROSAMARIA

Who?

CHICO

Can't you smell the burning? There is no time –

ANTÔNIO

I'm wasn't with them. The landowners who did that to you.

CHICO

This is no time to go back over old ground. Look around you, it's happening now. Listen. Can't you hear them? It's happening and you're doing nothing to stop them.

ANTÔNIO

I'm doing what I can for my family. For my daughter.

ROSAMARIA

She knows that...

CHICO

Don't you think I loved my son? My daughter? I did what I did for them.

ANTÔNIO

Leave me! Leave me! I cannot see you. I don't see you.

ROSAMARIA

(*Uncertain.*) Leave you? Yes, yes I am... I'm leaving you to find my friend.

CHICO

You must do something now.

ANTÔNIO

I must find my bull.

CHICO

Come now or everything will be lost.

ANTÔNIO

No!

> *CHICO attracts the attention of ANTÔNIO's horse and makes it gallop in the direction of the deforestation.*

ROSAMARIA

See you at the *quadrilha* tonight!

SCENE 11

The VAQUEIROS sing to the rhythm of their cutting down the forest.

Enter FRANCISCO with the BULL. CATARINA follows impatiently.

Duet.

FRANCISCO

Boi, easy now, *boi*,
You've had your last dance
Such a good boy,
But the time has come,
This is the end.
Boi, you're just a bull
And she is my wife,
Mother of my child,
Light, for better or worse,
Light of my life.

CATARINA

Quicker, Francisco, quicker,
Cut it and then pull!
Just bring me the tongue
Of the Master's prize bull.

FRANCISCO

Wife, dear wife of mine,
I still don't see
Why you want his tongue?
Stay calm,
Happy with me
And our child to be.

CATARINA

Because my baby needs it,
Or it will have no ears nor eyes!
Because my baby needs it,
Or surely it will die!
Because my baby needs it,
For new life to come from old!

Because my baby needs it,
So do what you are told!

FRANCISCO

Peace, easy *boi*, peace,
Lie in my arms now,
What a fine dance,
Boi, you're my best friend,
True to the end,
Boi, I'm letting you go.
But you will be
With me forever,
Light, for better or worse,
Light of my life.

CATARINA

Quicker, Francisco, quicker,
Cut the root then pull!
Just bring me the tongue
Of the master's prize bull!

Now Francisco now!
Do it for me NOW!

FRANCISCO kills the BULL and cuts out its tongue. CATARINA takes the still warm bloody tongue from him and eats it.

Exit FRANCISCO and CATARINA, leaving the carcass of the BULL.

Deafening sound of trees splintering and falling.

SCENE 12

The VAQUEIROS and RICARDO finally turn their chainsaws and axes to the Rainha da Mata *just as ANTÔNIO enters.*

ANTÔNIO

STOP!

RICARDO and ANTÔNIO face each other in the devastated forest.

RICARDO

Uncle, Uncle you have returned. So soon. Look, Uncle, is it not a thing of wonder? A hundred-acre farm turned into five-thousand-acre farm in one night? Look, look this way, you can see uninterrupted to the river, and that, you can see all the way to the next village. And there, the road to town. Now, now we'll knock down the villagers' old shacks and build a new barn, large enough to shelter during the wet season. A thousand – no two thousand – no, why not five? – five thousand cattle. If your bull is as good as you think he is, Uncle, he'll dance for us every year... And I've agreed a price with loggers for the wood and then, then when they have cleared it, the grass will start to grow! And we'll build ourselves a big new house with hot running water and air conditioning and electricity everywhere. You and me, Uncle, and get ourselves a big four-seater pick-up with air-conditioning and be able to drive from one side of the farm to the other under the midday sun. We won't need so many vaqueiros. In our pick-up you and me can do the herding, you and me... Uncle? Uncle? What do you think? Tell me what you think? Do you not think it a thing of wonder? Are you not happy? To see how big and broad your farm now is, how far it stretches? (*Pause.*) That we will now be rich and not have to worry about whether the bull dances or not. (*Pause.*) I only wanted you to be proud of me. To repay you for all you've done for me. Taken me in, raised me as your own, spent so much on my education. You've given me my life. And I want to bring new life to the our family, to the farm, to the village. Uncle?

ANTÔNIO

You have brought death to us all. Ricardo, Ricardo, you don't know what you have done.

VAQUEIRO discovers the BULL.

VAQUEIRO

No! It's impossible... Seu Antônio?!

ANTÔNIO looks up. The VAQUEIROS lift the carcass and lay it in front of ANTÔNIO. Some of them are weeping.

ANTÔNIO

What? What is this?

VAQUEIRO

The bull is dead. Its tongue has been ripped out.

ANTÔNIO

His tongue?

VAQUEIRO

Yes Master.

ANTÔNIO

No, no it's not dead. It cannot be. No. No. Never. Go, go fetch the doctor and the priest, they are knowledgeable men. He's sleeping. They'll know how to revive this bull.

Exit VAQUEIRO.

ANTÔNIO

And find me the man who did this to my *boi*. Find him!

RICARDO

Yes Uncle, I will, Uncle.

ANTÔNIO

And the rest of you, put on your costumes and your masks. Prepare yourselves and be ready in an hour's time. Tonight we will dance the *bumba meu boi* or my name's not Antônio Cícero Machado dos Santos Pinheiro e Pinheiro.

SCENE 13

Nearly dawn. The Forest.

TIA TEREZA

(*Sings.*) Moon shines in the dark,
Girl wakes by the river,
Danced and played all night long,
Entranced by the moonlight's song.

She's lost in the dark,
Wants his love for ever,
This girl must be strong,
Or be lost to the moonlight's song.

Enter ROSAMARIA. The BOTO appears.

ROSAMARIA

You came back to me, my love. O my love, my love I have it
all worked out. What is it? What is it?

ROSAMARIA's gaze follows that of the BOTO.

Yes, yes I know, something awful is happening the forest, but
we can save it, I found a way that we can be together forever –

The BOTO gently pushes her away.

All you have to do is stay a man, my love. I've found a way
for my father to accept you. You can come live with me and
be my love, my love. We can be together forever. Live here,
work here. It's amazing the things one can do dressed as a
man. Even if you stink!

Music.

(*Spoken.*) Just think my love,
What it would be like,
If you lived on dry land.
Just think my *Boto*
If you were to live like a man.

(*Sings.*) When you become a man,
You can smoke big cigars,
When you become a man,

79

You can drive the fastest cars.
When you become a man,
You can make a lot of money.
When you become a man,
You can be loud and funny.

You can flip,
You can flop,
In the water.
Kiss a fish,
That's delicious,
I am sure.
But the fun's
Just begun
When there's a woman in the plan.
And that's the fun you're going to have,
When you're a man.

You could crawl,
You could climb,
And you'll enjoy it.
You could fall,
You could jump,
And be my man.

You could talk,
You could walk,
You could run,
And run and run and run…
And that's the fun you're going to have,
When you're a man.

When you become a man,
You can smoke big cigars.
When you become a man,
You can drive the fastest cars.
When you become a man,
You can make loads of money.
When you become a man,
You can be loud and funny.

The BOTO breaks away from her.

What is wrong my Boto? Is it me? Don't you want to spend the rest of your life with me?

The BOTO turns away.

What are you saying? Tia Tereza, where are you? You got me into this –

TIA TEREZA

He's saying how can you ask him to live as a man, when man is capable of such destruction? Look up. Can't you see the smoke? Can't you hear what is coming?

The BOTO kisses ROSAMARIA, then goes to leave.

ROSAMARIA

Don't leave me. I don't want to live without you.

The BOTO holds out his hand.

What's he saying, Tia Tereza?

TIA TEREZA

You know what he's saying.

ROSAMARIA

(*Confused.*) To go with you? To live in the river? No. How could I, Tia Tereza? I am not a fish. What about my family?

TIA TEREZA

Yes, you'd miss them.

ROSAMARIA

They're all that I've known. And Catarina. She is like a mother to me. And the forest?

TIA TEREZA

Look at the forest –

The BOTO has returned to the river.

ROSAMARIA

No. Don't go. Please. Tia Tereza, what do I do?

TIA TEREZA

How much do you want him?

ROSAMARIA

More than anything.

TIA TEREZA

More than anything. Sometimes you must give up that which you know, for that which you know you must do.

ROSAMARIA

What do you mean?

TIA TEREZA

You're asking him to give up everything to become a man and live with you. What are you prepared to give up?

ROSAMARIA

Everything. I'd give up everything... But how?

TIA TEREZA

In that case there is another magic rhyme I know...

Exit TIA TEREZA and ROSAMARIA.

SCENE 14

Elsewhere in the ruined forest. FRANCISCO and CATARINA cling to each other in a devastated tree. Silence.

FRANCISCO

The hunger's passed?

CATARINA

Yes.

Pause.

FRANCISCO

That's good.

Beat.

CATARINA

Good? How is it good? O Chiquinho, what have I made you do?

FRANCISCO

I did it for you, Trina. I did it for you and our baby.

CATARINA

And now look at the forest. Did we do this?

Enter RICARDO.

RICARDO

Francisco? Where are you Francisco?

He cannot find FRANCISCO. Exit RICARDO.

CATARINA

They've found it, they've found the bull. Ricardo's out looking for us. What will he do to us?

FRANCISCO

To me. I take responsibility.

CATARINA

There'll be no bull dance, no *quadrilha*. What will become of the village? And what is that I can hear in the distance?

FRANCISCO

Hush my, prickly pear, you must rest. You need to save your energy for the baby.

CATARINA

What will become of us, Chiquinho? What will we do?

FRANCISCO

Hush.

> *FRANCISCO soothes CATARINA to sleep. FRANCISCO sees CHICO.*

Chico, Chico what have I done?

CHICO

You have given your beautiful wife the tongue of the bull so she might nurture new life in her womb.

FRANCISCO

But I killed the Master's bull.

CHICO

When the leopard dies in the heart of the forest, new trees spring up from his decomposing corpse. Everything must die so everything might live. Everything is connected to everything. The old bull must die so the new bull might rise from the cold ground. The village need the bull to dance, now more than ever. You must go back to help your community. You must discover why you are needed.

FRANCISCO

Me? But I'm not a bull, I'm just a frightened man. They've found the bull, the Master will kill me.

CHICO

To be afraid is human. To let fear rule us makes us less than we might be. I was frightened.

FRANCISCO

You?

CHICO

I was afraid to go back to my home knowing that the
landowners wanted to kill me. I knew that the police and the
government would not protect me.

FRANCISCO

Why? Why did they want to kill you? Who are you, Chico?

CHICO

It doesn't matter who I am. I was just someone who helped
bring life back to the people who lived in the forest. *Vaqueiros*,
seringueiros, Indians. Together we defended our lives here.

FRANCISCO

But I can't do anything like that

CHICO

You can bring life back to the bull. You can make him dance
again. And then you will be able to fight the other battles that
are coming.

FRANCISCO

Who are you? What are you?

CHICO

I knew they wanted to kill me, but still I came back, because
I knew that it was what I must do. Or the landowners, the
government and the police would have won. Fear would have
won. I went back for my wife and my children. You must go
back, Francisco. They're here again. Listen. Can't you hear
them coming? The developers and their diggers. What world
do you want for Catarina and your baby?

FRANCISCO

You're that Chico! You're Chico Mendes! But you're dead.

CHICO

There is a map of this forest on my heart. I will show you.

FRANCISCO

No don't, I don't want to see.

CHICO reveals bullet wounds around his heart.

85

But you're dead, you're a ghost! Why won't you rest in peace?

CHICO

How can I rest in peace when my heart is being destroyed bit by bit? You must go back, Francisco, you must revive the bull, you must revive the forest, you must revive your community. Everything is connected.

FRANCISCO

Me? I can't bring a bull back from the dead.

CHICO

But remember the sticks.

FRANCISCO

The sticks? How are sticks going to help a dead bull to dance? I can't. No. No, you're not real. I'm daydreaming again. I must grow up, stop daydreaming. I don't want to see you. I don't want to listen to you. Leave me alone.

CHICO

In that case –

CHICO whistles.

Over here.

CHICO whistles.

The man you're looking for is over here.

Enter RICARDO.

RICARDO

Who called? Who –?

RICARDO sees FRANCISCO.

SCENE 15

VILLAGERS stand around the dead BULL in their quadrilha *costumes. They are lost.*

ANTÔNIO

My *boi*! My *boi*! Do you see, my good friends, do you see what has happened to him while I was away in town? Call the doctor! Call the priest! They are the only ones who can save him now.

VILLAGERS call the DOCTOR and the PRIEST. Frantic.

DOCTOR arrives first.

Doctor, doctor. You must cure him. He must dance the *bumba meu boi* before the clock strikes twelve, so São João will bless us for the coming year. I beg you. Use your arts and your knowledge to cure him.

VILLAGERS

Cure him, doctor, cure him. Make him dance again, etc.

DOCTOR

But Seu Antônio, the…er…patient appears to be dead.

ANTÔNIO

I'll give you money. All the money I receive from these felled trees. They must be worth 10,000 dollars at least. 10,000 dollars if you cure my bull and make him dance before midnight.

DOCTOR

A handsome fee, Seu Antônio. And in that case I have full confidence that my mastery of medical science shall rise to the challenge. It has clearly suffered a temporary seizure or blockage, or a haemorrhage, or a case of bovine narcolepsy – May I, Seu Antônio?

ANTÔNIO

Please.

DOCTOR tries all sorts of procedures urged on by the crowd. Fails.

DOCTOR

In spite of the great reward offered, Seu Antônio, scientific reward that is, I am sorry to say that science has no cure for whatever it is that ails your bull.

He leaves hastily. Booed by crowd.

ANTÔNIO

Quack! Miserable failure! Doctors know nothing. Where's the Priest? Call the Priest! Only the Church can save us now! 10,000 dollars for the parish church if you can bring back my bull to dance.

Enter PRIEST.

PRIEST

Move aside, move aside. I think you'll find that resurrection is the preserve of the Church not medicine – and besides, my little church is greatly in need of a donation. The bull is clearly possessed by a lugubrious spirit or in a state of catatonic ecstasy or morbid communion.

PRIEST tries all sorts of procedures urged on by the crowd. Fails.

Though the Church could do with such a kind donation, religion – though it might be of some solace to you Seu Antônio – can offer no solution for a dead bull.

Exit PRIEST, followed by boos.

ANTÔNIO

What? Can no one wake my bull?

Enter RICARDO with the captive FRANCISCO, followed by CATARINA.

RICARDO

I found him Uncle, I found Francisco.

ANTÔNIO

Francisco? Francisco? Are you responsible for this?

FRANCISCO

I, I am, Seu Antônio.

CATARINA

He isn't, it's my fault.

FRANCISCO

No, Seu Antônio, it is my responsibility.

ANTÔNIO

I warned you, Francisco, I warned you that if my bull did not dance by midnight tonight I would make you dance on hot coals.

FRANCISCO

You did, Seu Antônio.

ANTÔNIO

And as sure as my name is Antônio Cícero Machado dos Santos Pinheiro e Pinheiro, I will see you dance on hot coals for this. Bring me red hot coals.

RICARDO

Yes, Uncle.

FRANCISCO breaks away and tries to flee. Great excitement. Shouts. The VILLAGERS try to stop him, he evades them. Finally CATARINA stops him.

FRANCISCO

Are you crazy? Let me go. What about the hot coals?

CATARINA

You can do it, Francisco. I believe in you.

CATARINA

Yes, *bobo*. You can do it. You climbed the tallest tree in the forest, you fought the *Cobra Grande*, you sacrificed your friend the bull for me and your baby... You are the only one that can now bring him back to life.

FRANCISCO

I can?

He takes a step towards the BULL.

ANTÔNIO

If the priest and the doctor could not do it, what hope have you, you fool? My bull is in this state because I trusted you to make him dance.

CATARINA

Seu Antônio, he's our last chance. Without him, the village will not survive.

FRANCISCO

Please Seu Antônio. Let me do it. I believe I can make him dance.

ANTÔNIO

Try then, while the coals are heating.

FRANCISCO goes up to the BULL. The VILLAGERS hold their breath.

FRANCISCO

(*Quietly.*) *Boi*? My bull? Wake up, my *boi*? This is your Pai Francisco. Like I told you, I'm going to be a daddy now. Wake up so I might one day get to see my son.

No response from the BULL. The VILLAGERS laugh.

Here, *boi*, I've got one for you. What do you call the two Argentinian firemen? José and Hose B.

No response from the BULL.

He's heard it before.

The VILLAGERS laugh.

ANTÔNIO

This is a waste of time.

FRANCISCO

I can't do this on my own, Chico. What did you mean about the sticks? One stick on its own is weak…

ANTÔNIO

What are you talking about?

FRANCISCO

But with a bunch –

Still not fully convinced, but desperate, FRANCISCO starts clapping and dancing. The VILLAGERS do not join in.

> Come my bull,
> Come King of the Union,
> Rise up from the cold ground,
> Come with God and our lady.
> Sing *bumba meu boi.*
> And dance, my bull, dance.

FRANCISCO dances and continues to clap and chant despite the laughter. FRANCISCO pulls CATARINA into the dance.

> Come my bull,
> Come King of the Union,
> Rise up from the cold ground,
> Come with God and our lady.

FRANCISCO pulls RICARDO into the dance.

> Sing *bumba meu boi,*
> And dance, my bull, dance.

The BULL twitches. The laughter stops. Some VAQUEIROS and VILLAGERS start to join in the chant and the dancing.

> Come my bull,
> Come King of the Union,
> Rise up from the cold ground,
> Come with God and our lady.
> Sing *bumba meu boi*
> And dance, my bull, dance!
> Dance my bull dance!
> Dance, my bull dance.

The BULL rises and dances. One by one the company joins them. As the dance draws to a close FRANCISCO and CHICO are left on stage.

FRANCISCO

I believed! I did something! I got others to do something with me!

Sound of the diggers is growing closer.

CHICO

This is just the beginning, Francisco. If you can bring the bull back to life then nothing is impossible for you and your village. Remember what I told you. Listen. Surely you can hear them now? It might be six months, it might be six years, but they are coming. And you can stop them.

FRANCISCO

But I'm just Francisco, who looks after the bull. We need you!

CHICO

No. You need each other. But I think you'll still be seeing me around these parts for some time to come. But hurry Francisco, it's still the Night of São João. And we've still got to dance the *quadrilha*.

FRANCISCO runs off and lights change.

SCENE 16

The quadrilha.

CHICO

(*On microphone.*) Ladies and gentlemen, the *Festa* São João would not be complete without the wedding *quadrilha*. And we still have a certain girl who is looking to marry the man of her dreams. Music Maestro!

Music. Enter the VAQUEIRO and SERINGUEIRA.

Please welcome the roughest, toughest, noblest cowboy in the land and his rubber-tapping *senhorita.*

Enter RICARDO on his own.

And now the Master's nephew, the one and only Seu Ricardo. But what's this? Does no one want to dance with him? Anyone? Can't have anyone left alone tonight. There must be someone for everyone. São João, there must be someone for everyone! And there, there is someone, a lonely fisherman waiting for a dance. Seu Pescador, come on in!

Enter PESCADOR to partner RICARDO.

As the Master says, this is an open-minded village is it not? And now, this year's king and queen of our São João *Festa,* the saviour of our bull, fearless Francisco and his wife the courageous Catarina –

Enter FRANCISCO and CATARINA who carries two newborn babies.

– and an extra special welcome to the future of Todos Os Santos and hope for all our future, their new twins, Chico and Chica! And so to the Master himself, Seu Antônio Cícero Machado dos Santos Pinheiro e Pinheiro. Who, I wonder, is there to partner him? Why the mother of moonlight, the lovely Tia Tereza herself of course.

Enter ANTÔNIO and TIA TEREZA.

But, this is a wedding and what do we need for a wedding?

CHICO takes suggestions from the audience.

A bride and groom of course. Ladies and gentlemen, a big
hand for…the groom!

*The BOTO is revealed dressed in immaculate morning suit, top
hat and cane.*

And, ladies and gentlemen, an even bigger hand for…the
magnificent, miraculous, mermaidious bride!

*ROSAMARIA is revealed as glorious Rio Carnival mermaid
bride.*

So let us dance the *quadrilha* and celebrate their wedding.

> (*Sung.*) Let's dance *quadrilha*,
> Dreaming Amazônia,
> And look for the love
> That will keep the world alive.
>
> Let's take our partners,
> Open up our hearts,
> And dance to play our part
> Now the forest is our bride.
>
> Let's dance *quadrilha*,
> Feel the rhythm in your
> Hearts and you will find,
> Amazônia for all time.
>
> There's still a chance now
> We can make a dance,
> And show that Amazônia
> Will keep the world alive.

*In the course of the dance ANTÔNIO, who is at first disapproving
of the BOTO, comes round to him when he sees how well he dances
and how much ROSAMARIA is in love with him. ROSAMARIA
and CATARINA make up with each other. ROSAMARIA dances
with CATARINA's babies. Perhaps RICARDO even begins to enjoy
dancing with the PESCADOR.*

CHICO

(*Spoken over the music.*) All the world's a stage, but the stage
cannot save the world. No single person can. This story is

not about us here in this country and them over there in Amazônia, it's about you and me, here and now. It's not about telling other people how to live their lives but about how we live our own lives in our own communities. Look after your own community, your own forests, your own parks and your own rivers. Fight for them and encourage those people with whom you live and love to protect your traditions, to preserve your environment and to care for your people. That's the way to send a message, by doing what you know you must do. And if sometimes you are afraid, that's fine, but do not give into fear. Live your lives as you know you should and be strong together. But most of all, keep dancing.

As the quadrilha *comes to an end, the BOTO and ROSAMARIA move towards the river.*

www.ingramcontent.com/pod-product-compliance
Ingram Content Group UK Ltd.
Pitfield, Milton Keynes, MK11 3LW, UK
UKHW031252020325
455690UK00007B/81